VANISHED CONNECTIONS

Unraveling Digital Disappearances, Serial Killers, True Crime, Cybercrime

Bella Novak

Table of Contents

Introduction

Shadows in the Digital Abyss

In the labyrinth of ones and zeros, where reality dissolves into lines of code and secrets are whispered through electronic pulses, a new breed of darkness emerges. Welcome to the realm where vanished connections cast long shadows, and the echoes of crimes committed in the virtual depths resonate with chilling clarity. Brace yourself, dear reader, for you are about to embark on a journey that will grip your imagination and plunge you headfirst into the digital abyss.

In "Vanished Connections: Unraveling Digital Disappearances," the boundaries between true crime and cybercrime blur, intertwining in ways that defy convention. Here, the battleground is the binary domain, and the adversaries are more elusive than ever—hackers, stalkers, and predators who hunt their prey not in the alleyways but in the ethereal landscapes of cyberspace. With every keystroke, every encrypted message, and every pixel of data, a new tale of mystery and danger unfurls.

Imagine a world where the hunt for a missing person begins not at the scene of a crime, but at the intersection of IP addresses and metadata. Visualize the detectives who don't just follow footprints in the sand but trace digital footprints across servers and networks, sifting through the debris of erased files and altered timestamps. In this realm, the race against time unfolds in microseconds, as clues vanish and new trails emerge in the blink of an eye.

But don't be fooled—the human element remains as potent as ever. Behind the screens, souls clash and destinies intertwine. Victims are lured by promises and threats, while predators employ psychological tactics that transcend the boundaries of the digital realm. The avatars they wear are masks of deception, concealing the darkness that thrives beneath. As you turn these pages, you will encounter survivors whose stories will touch your heart, law enforcement heroes who navigate the uncharted waters of virtual crime scenes, and experts who dissect the psychology of those who haunt the digital shadows.

The invisible becomes tangible, the virtual becomes real, and the digital age is a landscape where heroes and villains wage a battle that echoes across dimensions. As you immerse yourself in "Vanished Connections," prepare to feel the thrill of the chase, the surge of adrenaline, and the chilling realization that the barriers between us and the digital abyss are thinner than we ever dared to imagine.

With every turn of the page, you will descend further into the heart of the darkness, until you find yourself on the edge of your seat, held captive by the twists and turns that only the digital abyss can offer. Welcome to the gripping, heart-pounding world of "Vanished Connections." Your journey starts now.

Chapter 1: The Web of Deceit

The New Frontier of Crime: Unveiling the World of Cybercrime

In the age of the internet, where the world fits snugly in the palm of our hands and information is just a click away, there lies a shadowy underbelly, often overlooked. With the advancement of technology, crime has evolved, adapting and morphing into forms we'd once thought were the stuff of science fiction. Just as the Wild West had its outlaws and the industrial age its mobsters, our digital age has spawned a new breed of criminals—cybercriminals.

The internet, vast and boundless, offers not only the allure of knowledge and connectivity but also the cloak of anonymity. Within its intricate circuits and codes, a parallel world thrives—one where deception reigns, identities are stolen, lives are disrupted, and a new frontier of crime has emerged.

This chapter plunges into the depths of this digital abyss, shedding light on a world where bytes and bits can be as deadly as bullets. The Web of Deceit is not spun from silk but from strings of code, and those ensnared might find escape an elusive dream. Welcome to the new frontier of crime, a world where the line between reality and virtuality is perilously thin, and where every click might be a step into a trap. Welcome to the world of cybercrime.

The First Disappearance: A gripping case study of an individual who vanished without a trace from the digital landscape, leaving investigators baffled.

The First Disappearance

The world we live in is woven tightly with threads of digital connections, so much so that being digitally invisible seems implausible. Yet, as investigators would find out, it was not just possible but had already happened.

Liam Thompson, a 27-year-old software developer from San Francisco, was an epitome of the tech-savvy generation. Active across multiple online platforms – from the standard social media sites like Facebook and

Instagram to more niche forums dedicated to software development and open-source projects – Liam was as digitally present as anyone could be. But one day, this extensive digital footprint, just... vanished.

It began innocently enough. Friends noticed Liam hadn't posted anything on his usually bustling Twitter for a couple of days. His daily streaks on Snapchat were broken. Initially, most brushed it off thinking he might be on a digital detox, a fad popular among many to take a break from the constant noise of online platforms.

However, concerns arose when professional commitments started getting affected. Emails to Liam bounced back. His Github repositories, once brimming with daily updates, lay dormant. Co-workers, unable to get a hold of him for scheduled meetings, reached out to his family.

The Thompsons, a close-knit family, were equally clueless. Their last contact with Liam was a video call a week ago, and he seemed his usual cheerful self. With each passing day, the worry intensified. A missing person report was filed.

The local police, upon taking up the case, were baffled by the challenges it presented. There was no digital trace of Liam. His bank accounts were untouched, and his credit cards hadn't registered any recent transactions. His cell phone was off, and attempts to trace it came to naught.

Cybercrime experts were brought in. What they uncovered was both fascinating and chilling. It was as if Liam Thompson had executed a digital Houdini act. Every trace of him, from personal emails to even the most inconspicuous of online interactions, had been meticulously wiped clean. No records of browser history, no deleted files – nothing.

This was no ordinary case of a person going off-grid. This was methodical, planned, and executed with precision. As investigators delved deeper, they began to unravel layers of digital intrigue, cyber espionage, and a murky underbelly of the digital age most are oblivious to.

The mystery of Liam's disappearance was just the tip of the iceberg. What lay underneath was a tangled web of digital deception, crime, and an ominous glimpse into the vulnerabilities of our interconnected lives.

The First Disappearance was not just a case study; it was a harbinger of the complexities and vulnerabilities of the digital era. And as the narrative unfolds, the lines between the virtual and real world blur, leaving one to question the very fabric of digital identity and existence.

Liam Thompson: The Enigma of Digital Erasure

Liam Thompson was no ordinary software developer. A prodigy, he'd begun coding at the age of eight and by his early twenties, he was a recognized name in the open-source community. Respected by peers and headhunted by the biggest tech giants, he had chosen a more modest path, working for a San Francisco startup dedicated to creating cybersecurity solutions.

That choice, as events would unfold, may have played a pivotal role in his mysterious disappearance.

Liam's last known physical appearance was at a cybersecurity seminar where he'd delivered a compelling presentation on potential vulnerabilities in popular operating systems. It was not just the content but also his revelation that there existed undisclosed backdoors, which if exploited, could lead to unparalleled breachcs.

In the weeks leading up to his vanishing act, close friends and colleagues recounted odd occurrences. His apartment had been broken into, yet nothing was stolen. He had mentioned being followed on more than one occasion. And then there were the hushed phone calls, the conversations which he'd quickly end when someone walked into the room.

Forensic experts found traces of a highly sophisticated malware on his personal devices. This wasn't your everyday spyware but something that had yet to be cataloged—a new breed that erased its tracks as it operated. Had Liam become a target because of what he knew or what he had uncovered?

Diving deeper, the cyber-investigation unit discovered that Liam had been working covertly on a project he called "Pandora." Piecing together fragments from encrypted drives and cloud backups, it was evident that "Pandora" wasn't just another cybersecurity solution but potentially a tool, or a key, that could unlock or lock digital doors at will.

The ramifications were immense. In the right hands, it could be the ultimate protection mechanism. The race was on, not just to find Liam but to secure Pandora.

Every major intelligence agency across the globe was on alert. Theories abounded—was he kidnapped by a nefarious group wanting control over Pandora? Had he gone into hiding, fearing for his safety? Or was he coerced into becoming part of a larger, more sinister plot?

As days turned to weeks, the tech community rallied. Using the hashtag #FindLiam, a worldwide movement began. Vigils were held, online forums were buzzing with conspiracy theories, and amateur sleuths were trying to piece together the puzzle.

Liam's disappearance wasn't just a case of a missing person. It had morphed into a global event, a clash between the unseen forces of the cyber underworld and those who sought to maintain digital order. The Web of Deceit had ensnared its most intriguing prey yet, and the world watched, waiting for the next thread to unravel.

The Ephemeral Nature of the Digital Realm

The shockwaves of Liam's disappearance resonated not only among the tech circles but also reverberated throughout mainstream culture. Discussions on online privacy, digital rights, and the covert battles taking place in cyberspace became part of everyday conversations. Television specials, radio talk shows, and even classroom discussions analyzed the magnitude of the situation. Everyone had the same question: How could someone so deeply embedded in the digital world vanish so completely?

Weeks transformed into months, and the initial fervor began to wane. Yet for those deeply involved in the investigation, the urgency never diminished. Each day was a race against time.

The world of cybercrime is unique. Unlike traditional crimes, evidence in the digital realm is fleeting. Data can be encrypted, wiped, or even time-stamped to self-destruct. And with the vast ocean of information on the internet, searching for one clue was akin to finding a needle in a haystack.

One evening, in a dimly lit room in the heart of the FBI's cybercrime unit, a breakthrough occurred. A young analyst discovered a pattern—tiny blips of code that seemed to resonate with Liam's coding style. It was subtle, almost poetic. To an untrained eye, these were just mundane lines, but to those who knew Liam's work, it was a signature.

The traced code led them to a previously uncharted part of the dark web, a virtual maze of information. Hidden among vast troves of data was a message:

"Pandora was never meant for harm. To ensure it remains a protector and not a destructor, I've scattered its pieces. To those who seek balance in the digital world, find them. To those who seek power, a warning— some boxes are best left unopened."

No mention of Liam's whereabouts. No indication of his well-being. Just a cryptic message, leaving more questions than answers.

While many took the message as a sign that Liam was still alive and acting of his own accord, others weren't so sure. The ambiguity of the message, the choice of words—everything became a subject of speculation.

The search for Liam Thompson and Pandora's fragmented code became one of the most significant digital mysteries of the decade. It served as a stark reminder of the delicate balance in the vast web of cyberspace. The incident underscored the duality of the digital age—a tool for progress but also a weapon that could destabilize.

As the chapter on Liam's enigmatic disappearance comes to a close, it leaves us pondering the vulnerabilities and impermanence of our digital existences. In a world that's ever-evolving and where shadows play tricks, one thing became abundantly clear: in the vast digital realm, nothing is truly as it seems.

Chapter 2: Behind the Screen

Unmasking the Cyber Predator

In a world where relationships often begin with the swipe of a finger or a clicked "friend request," it's easy to forget the weight and reality of our digital interactions. Behind every profile picture, every witty bio, lurks a story—a human with dreams, fears, and intentions. While the majority engage in online communities with benign or friendly motives, there exists a sinister minority with far darker intentions. They are the shadows in the alleyways of the digital world: the cyber predators.

The Psychology of a Predator

The realm of the cyber predator is not too different from that of the traditional predator. Both hunt with a strategy, identify vulnerabilities, and strike when the time is right. However, the tools and tactics of a cyber predator are uniquely adapted to the digital environment, making them harder to identify and their actions harder to predict.

To understand the cyber predator's mind, one must first acknowledge the allure of anonymity. In the physical world, a predator must face the risk of being seen or identified. Online, behind the safety of a screen, they can be anyone: a friendly face, a confidante, or a passionate lover. This freedom from accountability emboldens them, allowing their darkest fantasies to take flight.

Many cyber predators experience a dissonance between their online and offline identities. The online world provides an escape, a space where they can wear a mask of their choosing without the weight of their real-world baggage. And as they become more invested in their digital personas, the lines between reality and fantasy blur, driving them deeper into their predatory habits.

The Art of Digital Manipulation

At its core, the act of online abduction or manipulation isn't about technology; it's about psychology. The cyber predator is a master manipulator, adept at reading cues and adapting their strategies accordingly.

In the early stages, they often present themselves as active listeners, offering a sympathetic ear to grievances and problems. By feigning empathy, they create an illusion of safety, urging their potential victims to let down their guards.

As the relationship progresses, the predator begins to introduce elements of control, often subtly. They might guilt-trip the victim for spending time with others or demand more personal information under the guise of deepening their connection. They use tools like flattery, promises, and even threats to ensure their victims remain ensnared.

Exploiting Vulnerabilities

Every individual has vulnerabilities. For many, it's a need for validation, for others, a longing for affection or understanding. Cyber predators have an uncanny ability to pinpoint these vulnerabilities and exploit them.

Teenagers and young adults, who are still shaping their identities and grappling with societal pressures, are particularly susceptible. A study found that cyber predators often look for individuals who display signs of loneliness, low self-esteem, or familial issues. These traits make them easier to manipulate and control.

But it's not just the young and impressionable who are at risk. Adults, especially those going through personal upheavals like divorces or midlife crises, can also fall prey. The predator offers them an illusion, a fantasy where they are valued, desired, and understood.

The online environment further amplifies these vulnerabilities. Social media platforms, with their emphasis on curated lives and perpetual happiness, can make individuals feel isolated and inadequate.

Predators capitalize on these feelings, presenting themselves as saviors or beacons of hope.

The Lure of the Unknown

There's an inherent thrill in the unknown, in connecting with a stranger and discovering their world. It's this very thrill that many predators weaponize. They present themselves as enigmas, luring their victims into a game of discovery.

For the victim, every revelation, every shared secret feels like a step closer to unraveling the mystery, not realizing that with every step, they're walking deeper into a carefully laid trap.

Protecting the Vulnerable

Awareness is the first line of defense. Recognizing the signs of manipulation and understanding the tactics employed by predators is crucial. Both parents and individuals must educate themselves about the dangers lurking behind the screen.

Open communication is key. Victims often keep their online relationships a secret, either out of fear of judgment or because they've been manipulated into doing so. By fostering an environment where open discussions about online interactions are encouraged, potential threats can be identified and addressed early on.

In addition, the use of technology to protect against these threats is crucial. Monitoring software, privacy settings, and regular check-ins on online activities can act as deterrents for predators.

Concluding Thoughts

The digital world, with all its conveniences and wonders, also harbors shadows that we must be wary of. Behind the screen, just as in the physical world, there are those who seek to harm and exploit.

The journey into the mind of a cyber predator is a chilling one, a testament to the depths of human depravity. However, by understanding their motives and tactics, society can arm itself, ensuring that the digital world remains a space of connection and not one of predation.

While technology evolves at a rapid pace, the basic tenets of trust, caution, and awareness remain unchanged. The onus is on each individual to safeguard themselves and their loved ones, ensuring that they navigate the online world with both wonder and caution.

The Dark Tangle of Social Media

In an era defined by instant connectivity, social media has emerged as a powerful tool for communication, networking, and self-expression. With platforms catering to every conceivable interest, from the latest dance trends to niche hobbies, the digital realm has ushered in unparalleled opportunities for global interaction. Yet, lurking behind the playful memes, glamorous selfies, and viral challenges lies a grim reality: social media has also become a hunting ground for cyber predators.

Social Media's Double-Edged Sword

One of the foundational appeals of social media lies in its democratizing power. Users, irrespective of their location, age, or socio-economic status, can connect, share, and build communities. These platforms allow us to present curated versions of our lives, and in many cases, they serve as a space for validation and affirmation. However, this curated nature also means that we often present an idealized version of reality, highlighting our vulnerabilities.

Predators exploit these vulnerabilities. By analyzing a person's posts, they can gauge their insecurities, passions, routines, and even family dynamics. With such profound insights into a potential victim's psyche, a predator is well-equipped to tailor their approach, making their advances seem genuine and alluring.

The Illusion of Familiarity

One of the key dangers on social platforms is the illusion of familiarity. Just because someone has a mutual friend or follows similar pages doesn't mean they are trustworthy. However, the very design of these platforms often blurs the distinction between friends and strangers.

For instance, when a friend 'likes' a comment or picture from someone we don't know, it might appear on our feed. These indirect interactions create an illusion of mutual connection, making it easier for a predator to initiate direct contact without raising suspicions.

The 'Follow' Culture

The new-age adage "more followers, more fame" has led to a concerning trend, especially among younger users. The pursuit of more 'followers' or 'friends' often translates to less scrutiny when accepting friend requests or followers. Predators capitalize on this trend, creating appealing profiles to gain access to potential victims. Once they're on a person's followers' list, they can closely monitor their posts, stories, and interactions, gathering information to use as bait.

Private Isn't Always Private

While most platforms offer privacy settings, ensuring that personal posts are visible only to a select audience, these settings are far from foolproof. Predators are often tech-savvy, utilizing workarounds to access content that users believe is 'private'. Furthermore, mutual connections might unknowingly share or screenshot content, providing predators with the information they seek.

Additionally, some platforms have features where 'public' and 'private' boundaries are ambiguous. Stories, location tags, and check-ins, even if intended for friends, can sometimes be accessed by a broader audience, making users unintentionally vulnerable.

Chatrooms and DMs: The Silent Snare

Direct messaging (DM) features on platforms offer a discreet channel for communication. For predators, this feature is invaluable. Initial interactions often start innocuously, with comments about shared interests or mutual friends. As conversations progress, they can take a darker turn, with the predator employing tactics like gaslighting, emotional manipulation, or blackmail.

Moreover, numerous platforms host chatrooms or groups based on interests. While many are harmless communities of enthusiasts, others can be fronts for predatory activities. Under the guise of shared passions, predators can initiate conversations with potential victims, slowly grooming and manipulating them.

The Subtle Art of Grooming

Grooming is a predatory tactic wherein the offender establishes a relationship or emotional connection with a potential victim to exploit them. On social media, this often starts with shared interests. A predator might feign enthusiasm for a hobby or express understanding about personal issues. Over time, they might introduce sexual topics or request personal information or pictures.

For many victims, especially younger ones, recognizing grooming can be challenging. The predator might be one of the few people who seem to 'understand' them, creating an emotional dependency. This bond ensures that even if a victim feels uncomfortable, they might not sever ties or report the predator.

Guarding Against the Dark Tangle

To navigate the labyrinthine world of social media safely, both awareness and proactive measures are crucial:

1. **Educate & Discuss**: Regular dialogues about online safety, especially with younger users, can

equip them to recognize and report suspicious behavior.

2. **Audit Privacy Settings**: Regularly review and update the privacy settings of all social media accounts. Ensure that personal information, location details, and posts are accessible only to trusted individuals.

3. **Think Before Sharing**: Before posting, consider the potential consequences. Is the post giving away too much information about routines, locations, or vulnerabilities?

4. **Validate Connections**: Before accepting friend requests or followers, validate the authenticity of the profile. Mutual friends or a high follower count don't necessarily vouch for credibility.

In Conclusion

Social media, in its essence, is a tool—a reflection of the intentions of its user. For every heartwarming tale of reconnection or newfound friendship, there's a darker narrative of exploitation and predation. Recognizing the perils and navigating the digital realm with caution ensures that social media remains a platform for genuine connection, not a web of deceit.

Recognizing the dangers is only the first step in a proactive journey towards safeguarding oneself and loved ones.

Verification Systems and their Limitations

Many platforms have begun to integrate verification systems, where certain profiles receive a badge or marker indicating their 'authenticity.' This is especially prevalent among celebrities or high-profile individuals. However, the everyday user should be wary of assuming that unverified profiles are inherently malicious or that verified ones are inherently benign. Predators can and have manipulated these systems, and an absence or presence of verification should never replace personal vigilance.

The Role of Algorithmic Echo Chambers

Social media algorithms are designed to cater to user preferences, showing them more of what they like or engage with. This creates an 'echo chamber' effect, where users are often exposed only to like-minded individuals or content. Predators can exploit these algorithmic tendencies. By aligning their content with a potential victim's interests, they can ensure that their profiles and posts appear more frequently on the victim's feed, establishing a sense of familiarity and trust.

Collaborative Vigilance: The Community's Role

Beyond individual measures, the broader online community has a role to play in ensuring safety. If a user encounters suspicious behavior, predatory tactics, or explicit threats, they should not only sever ties but also report it to the platform. Communities and groups can set guidelines for interactions and be vigilant about potential threats. A collective approach ensures that predatory behavior is flagged faster and addressed more comprehensively.

Forward Steps: The Role of Platforms

While user vigilance is paramount, social media platforms must also shoulder responsibility. Continuous refining of privacy settings, stricter regulations on content sharing, and more transparent algorithms can reduce risks. Features like time-stamped screenshots, two-factor authentication, and warnings about unsolicited links can deter predators. Platforms need to prioritize user safety over engagement metrics, ensuring that their spaces remain conducive to genuine, safe interactions.

Final Thoughts

The intertwining of our lives with the digital realm is inevitable and, in many ways, beneficial. However, as with any tool, its utility is defined by its usage. Social media can be a window to the world, a platform for self-expression, and a bridge to distant friends. But, its dark tangle underscores the need for caution.

It's imperative to strike a balance: embracing the possibilities offered by social media, while being acutely aware of its pitfalls. Knowledge, vigilance, and collective responsibility will ensure that the digital frontier remains a space of connection, not exploitation.

Chapter 3: Chasing Shadows

The world of cybercrime is a dynamic, ever-shifting landscape. It's a realm where predators are always one step ahead, leaving faint trails and elusive clues. This chapter dives into the chase, the relentless pursuit of these virtual shadows by investigators, cybersecurity experts, and victims themselves.

From Bytes to Footprints: The Digital Trail

Every online action leaves behind a trace, a piece of digital evidence. For investigators, these are the footprints that guide the chase. From IP addresses to browser histories, these trails, however faint, can provide crucial leads.

However, cybercriminals employ a range of tactics to mask their online movements. They might use Virtual Private Networks (VPNs) to mask their IP addresses or deploy malware that erases their digital footsteps. The chase becomes a game of cat and mouse, with investigators using sophisticated software to unmask the elusive prey.

The Challenge of Jurisdiction

One of the unique challenges in chasing cybercriminals is the issue of jurisdiction. The digital realm knows no borders. A predator in Eastern Europe can target a victim in North America with the same ease as one in their own city. This global reach complicates the chase.

Laws and regulations vary between countries, and international cooperation can be slow and riddled with bureaucratic hurdles. Moreover, certain countries may become safe havens for cybercriminals, either due to lax regulations or because they become hubs for cybercrime syndicates.

Unmasking Anonymous: The Dark Web Challenge

The Dark Web, a segment of the internet hidden from standard search engines and requiring specific software to access, is a sanctuary for cybercriminals. It's a marketplace for illegal goods, including stolen data, drugs, and even human trafficking.

Chasing shadows in the Dark Web is like navigating a labyrinth in the dark. The standard rules don't apply here. Transactions are often made using cryptocurrencies, ensuring anonymity for both buyer and seller. Moreover, websites on the Dark Web frequently change their addresses to avoid detection, adding another layer of complexity to the chase.

Victim-Predator Dynamics: A Double-Edged Sword

In some cases, victims, driven by a desire for justice or closure, may try to chase down their attackers. This can be a double-edged sword. On one hand, victims may possess unique insights into the predator's tactics or psychology, aiding the pursuit. On the other hand, an emotionally-charged chase can lead to recklessness, potentially endangering the victim further.

It's a delicate balance, one that underscores the importance of collaboration between victims, law enforcement, and cybersecurity experts.

Collaborative Pursuits: Communities against Shadows

In recent years, online communities dedicated to tracking and exposing cybercriminals have emerged. These communities, often comprised of cybersecurity experts, victims, and everyday netizens, work collectively to chase down these digital shadows.

Platforms like forums, blogs, and even social media groups have become hubs for sharing information, comparing notes, and pooling resources. They exemplify the power of collective action against a common adversary.

Innovations in the Chase: New-Age Solutions

As cybercriminals evolve, so do the tools and techniques to chase them down. Machine learning algorithms can now predict patterns of malicious activity, and artificial intelligence-driven software can analyze vast datasets rapidly, spotting anomalies that might indicate predatory behavior.

Blockchain technology, often associated with cryptocurrencies, can also be leveraged to create transparent, immutable records, making it harder for criminals to mask their activities.

The Eternal Chase

Chasing shadows in the digital realm is a relentless endeavor. It's a pursuit marked by highs and lows, victories and setbacks. But, it's a necessary one. As long as there are shadows lurking in the cyber corners, there will be those dedicated to chasing them down, ensuring that the digital realm remains a space of safety and connection.

The hope is that, with time, technological advancements, and collaborative efforts, the chase will tilt in favor of the pursuers, casting light on the darkest corners of the cyber world.

Digital Footprints and Dead Ends:

The intricate web of the internet is filled with traces of our online presence—digital footprints that document our interactions, interests, and movements. But like footprints on a sandy shore, these traces can be fleeting, washed away by the incessant tide of data or deliberately obscured by those keen to remain hidden. For law enforcement agencies, navigating this digital labyrinth can be both a treasure hunt and a chase filled with dead ends.

Understanding Digital Footprints

Every click, search query, social media interaction, or online transaction leaves a trace—a digital footprint. These can be broadly categorized into two types:

1. **Active Footprints**: These are deliberately left behind when users share information online, such as social media posts, uploaded photos, or blog articles.

2. **Passive Footprints**: These are created without the user's explicit action, like browser cookies, IP logs, or location data shared by mobile apps.

Both footprints are invaluable for investigators. They paint a picture of a person's habits, preferences, and associations, providing crucial leads.

The Initial Pursuit: Low Hanging Fruit

When embarking on an investigation, detectives first delve into the more apparent traces. Social media platforms are a goldmine. Even if a user has recently deactivated their account or deleted certain posts, platforms often retain this data for a period, which can be accessed with the appropriate legal permissions.

Search histories can reveal a lot about a person's mindset, fears, or intentions. Were they looking for information on disappearing without a trace? Were there recent searches indicating distress or a plan to travel?

However, as one might expect, those intent on disappearing or committing cybercrimes often take measures to erase or manipulate these obvious trails.

VPN and Encryption: The Veils of the Digital World

The use of Virtual Private Networks (VPNs) and encryption tools has grown significantly. While they serve legitimate purposes like maintaining privacy or bypassing geo-restrictions, they're also used by individuals wanting to evade detection.

VPNs mask the original IP address, making it appear as though the user is accessing the internet from a different location. Encryption tools, on the other hand, scramble data, rendering it unreadable without the correct decryption key.

These tools present formidable barriers, turning clear trails into mazes. But they're not insurmountable. With the right expertise and resources, encrypted data can sometimes be decrypted, and VPNs can be bypassed, albeit with significant effort.

Deep Dive: Into the Dark Web

The Dark Web is a part of the internet inaccessible through standard browsers. Often, when standard digital trails run cold, the path leads investigators here.

Transactions on the Dark Web are designed to be untraceable, with users often employing cryptocurrencies. But the very features that ensure anonymity—like the reliance on specific browsers to access the Dark Web or unique transaction IDs for cryptocurrency exchanges—can be exploited by law enforcement to trace activities.

Data Forensics: The Science Behind the Search

As cybercriminal activities evolve, so do the methods to track them. Data forensics experts specialize in retrieving, preserving, and analyzing digital evidence. This involves:

1. **Retrieving Data**: Even deleted data can often be recovered. When a file is 'deleted,' it's not immediately removed from the storage medium; instead, its space is marked as available. Until that space is overwritten by new data, recovery is possible.

2. **Analyzing Metadata**: Metadata is the data about data. For instance, a photo's metadata might reveal the device it was taken on, the time and date, or even the location.

3. **Cloud Traces**: Many devices automatically back up to cloud storage. Accessing this can

provide a treasure trove of information, from saved messages to location history.

Collaboration Across Borders

Given the global nature of the internet, collaboration between international law enforcement agencies is vital. Organizations like INTERPOL have specialized cybercrime units that facilitate this collaboration, ensuring that digital footprints, which might span multiple countries, are pursued seamlessly.

However, geopolitical considerations, differing legal frameworks, or bureaucratic red tape can sometimes hinder this collaborative pursuit.

The Role of Tech Companies

On one hand, they're committed to protecting user privacy. On the other, they're under pressure to assist law enforcement.

Over the years, there have been several high-profile standoffs between tech companies and law enforcement agencies over access to encrypted data. The outcome often depends on legal battles, public opinion, and the specific circumstances of the case.

Dead Ends and New Beginnings

The pursuit of digital footprints is filled with both breakthroughs and frustrations. A promising lead might suddenly hit a wall, like an encrypted device that resists all efforts to unlock it or a trail that disappears into the vastness of the Dark Web.

But for every dead end, new paths often emerge. An overlooked social media post, a witness who noticed a seemingly inconsequential detail, or advancements in data forensics tools can reignite a stalled investigation.

A Race Against Time

The quest to trace digital footprints in the vast expanse of the internet is a race against time. With every passing moment, digital trails risk being overwritten, erased, or obscured. Yet, it's a testament to the determination of law enforcement agencies and the rapid advancements in technology that many who vanish into the digital ether are eventually found.

As the digital realm expands and evolves, so will the challenges in tracing these footprints. But so too will the tools, techniques, and collaborative efforts to ensure that even in the vast, shadowy corridors of the internet, few can disappear without a trace.

The Vigilante Hackers:

In the vast digital expanse, amidst the code, data streams, and intricate networks, a unique breed of hackers operates. Unlike those who delve into the world of cybercrime, these individuals use their formidable skills for good. Often unsanctioned, sometimes controversial, but undeniably effective, they are the vigilante hackers. This subsection delves into their world, shedding light on the unsung heroes of the digital realm.

Introduction to White Hat Hackers

Before exploring vigilante hackers, it's essential to understand the broader spectrum of ethical hacking. At one end are the 'White Hat' hackers—professionals employed to identify and fix vulnerabilities in systems. They operate entirely within the bounds of the law, often working for major corporations or government agencies to strengthen cyber defenses.

Into the Gray Zone: Vigilante Hackers

Vigilante hackers operate in a gray zone. While their intentions align with the White Hats—protecting the innocent and thwarting the malicious—their methods often fall outside formal legal frameworks. Without official sanction, they embark on missions to expose, disrupt, or dismantle cyber threats.

Notable Operations

1. **Operation Darknet**: A group of vigilante hackers took on child pornography rings operating within the Dark Web. By infiltrating their networks, these hackers not only shut down multiple sites but also publicly exposed thousands of users, leading to numerous arrests.

2. **Project Chanology**: Initiated by the loosely associated group 'Anonymous', this operation targeted the Church of Scientology, exposing its alleged cyber-censorship efforts and other controversial activities.

3. **Hunting Terrorist Networks**: Various vigilante hackers have turned their sights on terrorist networks, particularly their online recruitment and propaganda channels. By hacking websites,

forums, and social media accounts, they've disrupted these operations and provided valuable intelligence to authorities.

The Morality and Ethics Debate

The actions of vigilante hackers invariably raise ethical questions. While many laud their efforts, especially when they achieve results where official channels fall short, others raise concerns about accountability, oversight, and potential collateral damage.

- **Privacy Concerns**: By operating outside legal bounds, there's no oversight ensuring the rights of individuals are preserved.

- **Potential for Mistakes**: Without a structured system of checks and balances, errors can occur, potentially targeting innocent parties.

- **Undermining Legal Processes**: Some argue that unsanctioned hacks could compromise official investigations or be used as a defense by cybercriminals in court.

Building Bridges: Collaboration with Law Enforcement

Recognizing the unique skills and insights of vigilante hackers, some law enforcement agencies have begun to collaborate unofficially. By leveraging the expertise of these digital warriors, while ensuring their operations adhere to legal frameworks, a middle ground can be found. Such collaborations can be exceptionally potent, combining the agility and innovation of vigilante hackers with the resources and authority of official agencies.

The Dangers and Sacrifices

Vigilante hacking isn't without personal risks. Cybercriminal networks, especially those linked to organized crime or extremist groups, can retaliate violently. Many vigilante hackers, therefore, maintain strict anonymity, not just to evade legal repercussions but to protect themselves and their loved ones.

Beyond physical dangers, there are legal risks. Operating in that gray zone means they're potentially one misstep away from prosecution. Their unwavering commitment, in the face of these challenges, underscores their dedication to the greater good.

Conclusion: The Digital Knights

In the age-old battle between good and evil, the digital realm has its knights—the vigilante hackers. Armed with keyboards, code, and an unwavering belief in justice, they challenge the shadows of the internet. Their methods might be unconventional, their operations unsanctioned, but their impact is undeniable. As the cyber landscape evolves, these vigilante hackers will undoubtedly continue to play a crucial, if controversial, role in safeguarding the digital frontier.

Chapter 4: The Virtual Crime Scene

As technology advances, so does the nature of crime. The traditional tape-bound crime scene has now expanded into the vast virtual realm. Within this expanse, perpetrators leave a different set of footprints, clues encrypted in code or buried deep within vast data fields. And unlike the real world, where time can be forgiving, the virtual arena is a race against the clock, where evidence is transient and can disappear in a digital heartbeat.

Cryptic Clues and Hidden Messages

In the annals of cybercrime history, there have been numerous instances where criminals, either due to arrogance, desire for recognition, or pure psychological compulsion, left clues in the digital world—breadcrumbs for investigators to find and decode.

1. **The Binary Signature**: In one notorious hacking incident, a hacker infiltrated several high-profile databases, leaving behind a signature in binary. When translated, it read, "Catch me if you can." The audacity of this signature ignited a furious manhunt, with investigators diving deep into the cyber underbelly. This binary clue would eventually lead to the hacker's unique coding style, acting as a digital fingerprint.

2. **The Digital Riddle**: In a case of cyber extortion, an anonymous criminal demanded a hefty ransom from a corporation. Instead of merely providing a cryptocurrency wallet for payment, the perpetrator sent a series of puzzles, each leading to subsequent clues about the payment method. While the intention might have been to elude capture by complicating the payment trail, the intricacy of the puzzles provided investigators with insights into the criminal's mindset and background.

3. **Secret Communications**: Some criminals have used hidden channels within seemingly innocent online platforms to communicate. Steganography, a method where messages are hidden within images or videos, has been employed. Detecting such hidden messages requires keen eyes and sophisticated tools. One breakthrough came when an investigator noticed a slight pattern anomaly in an image, leading to the discovery of a hidden chat log.

These clues, while tantalizing, also showcase the evolution of cybercrime. The cat-and-mouse game between criminals and investigators has become a complex dance of intellect, innovation, and intuition.

The Race Against Time

Unlike the physical world, where fingerprints might last for years or DNA can be preserved, the digital realm is inherently ephemeral. Data can be overwritten, servers shut down, and entire digital identities erased in moments.

1. **The 48-Hour Window**: Experts often refer to a critical 48-hour window post a cybercrime incident. This period is crucial for gathering volatile data, such as RAM contents, temporary files, or recent network connections. After this window, the chance of retrieving this data diminishes drastically.

2. **Remote Wipe-Outs**: Criminals with advanced knowledge can remotely wipe their tracks. If they sense they're being pursued or their operations compromised, with a few commands, they can initiate protocols to delete evidence, further complicating investigations.

3. **Jurisdictional Challenges**: The global nature of the internet means evidence can be housed on servers across international borders. Securing this evidence before it's deleted requires swift

collaboration between nations, often fraught with bureaucratic delays.

Yet, in this high-pressure race, law enforcement agencies have also adapted. Rapid response cyber units, real-time data capture tools, and international cybercrime treaties have all been established to ensure that the ticking clock of the virtual world doesn't impede the pursuit of justice.

A New Age of Investigation

The virtual crime scene represents the next frontier of criminal investigation. It's a realm where the clues are coded, the footprints are digital, and the clock never stops ticking. As criminals evolve, so too must the strategies and tools used to pursue them. In this endless chase, one thing remains constant: the relentless pursuit of justice, whether in the tangible world or the vast expanse of the virtual realm.

Chapter 5: Unraveling the Code

Cyber Profilers: Inside the Minds Behind the Screens

Picture this: Late at night, in a dimly lit room filled with the hum of computers, someone's fingers dance over a keyboard. They're on a mission, but it's not to save a virtual world or to finish up some work. They're navigating the intricate pathways of the dark web, breaking into databases, or perhaps devising a new malware to unleash on the world. This is the domain of the digital criminal.

Now, imagine another scene. In a bright office filled with whiteboards covered in scribbles, charts, and diagrams, a group of experts pores over a maze of digital data. They're not just looking for code anomalies or breaches—they're searching for patterns, trying to get into the mindset of the individual behind that cybercrime. Welcome to the world of the cyber profiler.

Who Are These Digital Detectives?

Cyber profilers aren't your average IT professionals. These experts specialize in understanding the human aspect behind cyber attacks. Think of them as the digital realm's equivalent of criminal profilers in the physical world. Just as forensic psychologists might analyze a crime scene to determine a perpetrator's motivations, these digital detectives interpret online actions to understand what drives cybercriminals.

Deciphering The Digital Signature

For instance, a hacker who leaves behind a calling card might be seeking recognition, while another who methodically covers their tracks might be motivated by paranoia or a deep-seated need for secrecy and control. By understanding these nuances, a cyber profiler can predict potential future targets and even suggest ways to engage or deter the criminal.

The Psychology of The Digital Abyss

It's fascinating to realize that the world wide web, vast and intangible, can be a mirror reflecting the deepest recesses of the human psyche. Some hackers are driven by political ideologies, seeking to right what they perceive as societal wrongs. Others might be motivated by past personal traumas, using their skills as a form of empowerment. And then there are those who are in it just for the thrill, the adrenaline rush of outsmarting systems and leaving a digital world in disarray.

Understanding these motives isn't just an academic exercise. It's crucial for defense. If you can predict a cybercriminal's next move, you can preemptively counteract it.

Empathy: The Unexpected Tool

One might think that the world of cybersecurity is cold and clinical, purely about codes, firewalls, and algorithms. But at the heart of the cyber profiler's toolkit is a deeply human skill: empathy. By placing themselves in the shoes of the hackers, by feeling their drives and understanding their desires, these profilers can weave a narrative around the lines of code left behind. It's this narrative that often holds the key to solving or preventing cyber crimes.

In the vast and ever-evolving landscape of the digital world, where codes can be rewritten and identities can be masked, the human element remains a constant. It's this very element that cyber profilers tap into, bridging the gap between technology and psychology. As we continue to navigate the challenges of the digital age, these experts remind us that behind every byte, behind every screen, lies the most intricate code of all: the human soul.

The Digital Autopsy:

In today's hyper-connected world, our online actions, intentional or not, often leave behind digital footprints. These traces, though intangible, can be as revealing as physical evidence at a crime scene. When someone mysteriously disappears or falls victim to an online predator, it's these digital remains that experts turn to, conducting what's known as a "digital autopsy."

Unlike the traditional autopsy, which examines a body to deduce cause of death and other vital information, a digital autopsy delves into a person's online history, searching for clues that might unravel the circumstances of their disappearance. This can involve scrutinizing a vast array of data: from email communications, social media interactions, and browsing histories, to more covert traces like metadata embedded in photos or files.

Every action taken online, no matter how insignificant it might seem at the moment, has the potential to become a vital clue in these investigations. For instance, a single search query made days or even weeks before a person's disappearance could provide insights into their state of mind or hint at potential threats they were facing. Analyzing patterns in communication can also be telling. A sudden drop in messaging frequency, or a notable change in tone or content, can be indicative of duress or a significant life event. Even passive online actions, like the websites a person frequents or the online groups they're part of, can paint a vivid picture of their interests, fears, and affiliations.

But as enlightening as these digital traces can be, they also present challenges. With the rise of encrypted communication and the increasing awareness around digital privacy, many are taking steps to minimize their online footprint. This can make the task of digital autopsy all the more complex. Yet, despite these challenges, the importance of digital autopsies in modern investigations can't be overstated. As our lives become increasingly intertwined with the digital realm, understanding the stories these virtual trails tell will only become more crucial in the quest for truth and justice.

Chapter 6: The Hunt for Justice

The digital realm, vast and intricate, has reshaped the world of crime and the subsequent pursuit of justice. It has transformed bedrooms into potential crime scenes, and screens into gateways of deception, extortion, and violence. As cybercriminals constantly evolve their methods, staying one step ahead of law enforcement, the game of cat and mouse becomes ever more complex. Yet, with collaboration, determination, and technological advancement, justice often prevails.

From Pixels to Handcuffs:

There's an adage in the world of cyber investigations: "Every click is a clue." Each action a criminal takes online leaves a digital trace, and it's these traces that law enforcement agencies worldwide use to piece together their cases.

The Pursuit of Evgeniy Bogachev

One of the most notorious instances of cybercriminal pursuit involves Evgeniy Bogachev. Known by his online moniker "lucky12345," Bogachev was behind the GameOver Zeus botnet, a network of compromised computers that he used to steal over $100 million from bank accounts worldwide. While his technical prowess was undeniable, what made him especially challenging to apprehend was his ability to continually evolve his tactics and maintain layers of anonymity.

After his crimes came to light, a massive multinational effort began to locate and apprehend Bogachev. The FBI collaborated with law enforcement agencies from various countries, tech companies, and cyber security firms. Together, this diverse team was able to dismantle the GameOver Zeus botnet. But Bogachev, being based in Russia and allegedly having ties to the Russian government, has yet to be apprehended. This instance highlights both the successes and challenges inherent to international cybercrime investigations.

Darknet Takedowns and International Collaborations

The Darknet, a part of the internet accessible only through specific software and known for its anonymity, is a hotspot for illegal activities. One of the most significant takedowns in its history was that of the AlphaBay and Hansa marketplaces in 2017. These platforms facilitated the sale of illegal drugs, weapons, and various other illicit items.

The operation to dismantle these marketplaces was a masterclass in international cooperation. Led by the FBI and the DEA, agencies from Thailand, the Netherlands, Lithuania, Canada, the UK, and France participated. After seizing AlphaBay, law enforcement monitored the exodus of its users to Hansa, which they had covertly taken control of. This allowed them to gather substantial amounts of intelligence on dealers and buyers, leading to numerous arrests and the disruption of criminal networks.

The Globe-spanning Effort

Such multinational collaborations aren't just confined to big operations. Every day, law enforcement agencies across the world share intelligence, tools, and resources to combat cyber threats. From forums peddling stolen credit card information to ransomware attacks paralyzing entire city infrastructures, the response is increasingly global.

Interpol's Cybercrime Directorate is a testament to this collective approach. With a focus on training, support, and operations, it provides a platform for countries to work together, bridging gaps in knowledge, resources, and jurisdictional challenges. The 24/7 Interpol Global Complex for Innovation in Singapore acts as a hub, assisting in real-time during cyber threats and attacks.

The Complexities of Extradition

One of the significant challenges in pursuing international cybercriminals is extradition. Different countries have varied stances on cybercrime and varying legal frameworks, making the process of extradition complicated. The notorious case of Gary McKinnon, a British hacker who broke into 97 U.S. military and NASA computers between 2001 and 2002, serves as a prime example. U.S. authorities wanted to extradite him for trial, but after a decade-long legal battle, the UK Home Secretary blocked the extradition, citing health concerns.

The hunt for justice in the realm of cybercrime is a multifaceted challenge. It requires cutting-edge technology, a deep understanding of the digital world, and a level of collaboration between countries that transcends politics and borders. While there are undeniable successes, the evolving nature of cybercrime means that law enforcement agencies must continually adapt, learn, and collaborate. From pixels to handcuffs, the journey is arduous, but the quest for justice remains unwavering.

The Ethical Dilemma:

The sprawling landscape of the digital age has brought forth a myriad of opportunities, but with them, new challenges. One of the most contentious topics arising from this landscape is the role of vigilante justice in the digital realm. As cybercrimes proliferate and victims grow in numbers, there's an increasing presence of self-appointed guardians in cyberspace who are willing to take matters into their own hands. But this raises a question: Is vigilante justice in the digital age a necessary force for good or a problematic overreach that undermines the legal system?

A Rise in Digital Vigilantes

Digital vigilantes, often with advanced technical skills, can operate from anywhere. Some are driven by a sense of justice, others by personal vendettas, and some simply by the thrill of the hunt. They expose online predators, track down hackers, and in some cases, even dox — or publicly reveal personal information about — individuals they deem to be 'wrongdoers'.

We've seen instances where these vigilantes have yielded positive results. For example, groups like Anonymous have often taken up causes, launching cyber-attacks against organizations they perceive to be acting unethically. They've exposed child predators, brought attention to injustices, and in some cases, have provided crucial information to law enforcement.

Overstepping Boundaries

However, the actions of digital vigilantes are not without criticism. By operating outside the legal framework, there's a risk of infringing on privacy rights, misidentifying innocent individuals, and inadvertently causing harm. The case of Sunil Tripathi serves as a grim reminder. Wrongly accused by online communities of being involved in the Boston Marathon bombing, the misidentification led to severe harassment and trauma for his family.

Furthermore, even when the vigilantes correctly identify wrongdoers, their methods can compromise official investigations. Evidence gathered through hacking or other illicit means might be inadmissible in court, potentially leading to legal loopholes that perpetrators can exploit.

Legal Implications

Beyond the immediate consequences, there's the broader question of how the legal system should approach digital vigilantes. Should they be prosecuted for their illicit activities, or should exceptions be made when their intentions are to serve a broader good? And where does one draw the line?

There's also the danger of encouraging a culture where individuals take the law into their own hands, leading to a decentralized and chaotic form of justice. Legal systems, with all their flaws, are built upon centuries of jurisprudence, designed to ensure that the accused are granted a fair trial and that evidence is gathered and presented in a structured manner.

Striking a Balance

There's no denying that digital vigilantes sometimes fill a gap, especially in cases where traditional law enforcement lacks the resources or expertise to act swiftly. Their actions, driven by a mix of altruism and expertise, can be a formidable force against cybercriminals. However, a system where individuals operate based on personal judgments, outside of any regulated framework, is fraught with dangers.

As the digital realm continues to grow, there's a pressing need to strike a balance. Collaborative models, where skilled individuals work in tandem with law enforcement, could be a potential way forward. By providing a legitimate platform for these individuals to contribute, we can harness their skills while ensuring that the rule of law is upheld.

In the end, the debate over digital vigilante justice touches upon broader themes of justice, ethics, and the evolving nature of our digital society. As technology continues to shape our interactions and our understanding of right and wrong, society must grapple with these complexities and navigate a path that upholds both justice and ethical integrity.

Chapter 7: Beyond the Binary

In the sprawling expanse of the digital realm, there exists a distinctive boundary, a precipice where the virtual merges with reality. It is a point of convergence, where bytes and pixels manifest into tangible consequences, where online actions culminate in real-world repercussions. This chapter ventures into that nexus, drawing back the curtain on the moments when cybercriminals, having operated in the seemingly intangible domain of the web, are forced to confront the weight of their actions in brick-and-mortar courtrooms.

From Digital to Reality

The Scene

Darkened rooms illuminated by the glow of computer screens, the rhythmic clatter of keystrokes, encrypted chats, and layers of anonymity—this is the stereotypical environment from which many cybercrimes emerge. The criminals often feel invincible, shielded by the vastness of the internet and the assumed security of their digital fortresses.

But the transition from this setting to the stark, fluorescent-lit hallways of a courthouse is jarring. The very nature of the internet, with its ephemeral sense of reality, stands in stark contrast to the palpable gravity of a courtroom. Here, the weight of evidence, the gaze of a jury, and the finality of a judge's gavel bring home the realization: the digital world's actions have profound real-world implications.

The Revelations

Imagine the case of a prolific hacker, known online by a cryptic pseudonym, finally unmasked and standing before a judge. In the shadows of the web, he might have been a feared entity, but in the courtroom, he's just another defendant, stripped of his digital cloak.

There's also the visceral impact on the victims. In many cases, their first real glimpse of the perpetrator is in court. While they've felt the repercussions of the crime—whether it's identity theft, online harassment, or a breached intimate space—the actual confrontation with the perpetrator is a poignant moment. It's a culmination of fears, anxieties, and the hope for justice.

Notable Cases

Consider the case of Ross Ulbricht, the mastermind behind Silk Road, an infamous dark web marketplace for illicit goods. In the digital realm, he went by the pseudonym "Dread Pirate Roberts," an almost mythical figure in the underground world. But when he was apprehended and subsequently tried, the courtroom drama laid bare the man behind the moniker—a young individual, not an omnipotent entity, facing the weighty consequences of his actions.

Then there's the story of the WannaCry ransomware attack, which paralyzed numerous systems globally, demanding ransoms and creating chaos. When Marcus Hutchins, a young British security researcher, identified a "kill switch" for the ransomware, he was hailed a hero. However, his subsequent arrest for earlier malware-related activities brought to light the complexities of the digital realm. The courtroom became a stage, laying bare the grey areas and moral ambiguities of the cyber world.

A Realm of Consequences

Beyond the drama, the courtroom serves as a poignant reminder that the internet isn't an abstract, consequence-free playground. Every action, every keystroke can have far-reaching repercussions. And while the digital age has brought along challenges that are often abstract and complex, the foundational principles of justice, accountability, and consequences remain as tangible as ever.

In closing, as we bear witness to these courtroom confrontations, it's a reflection on the broader theme that permeates this book: the interplay between the digital and the tangible, between bytes and reality. In the end, even in the vastness of cyberspace, one cannot escape the age-old tenets of right and wrong, of actions and consequences.

Impact and Redemption:

In a world seamlessly interwoven with digital threads, the ripples of cybercrime are felt far beyond the confines of screens and servers. For many, the ramifications echo through their lives, changing their perceptions of trust, security, and the very nature of human interaction in an interconnected world. But amidst the tales of trauma and violation, there also emerge powerful narratives of resilience, redemption, and a tenacious human spirit that refuses to be defined by victimhood.

The Lingering Shadows of Digital Crime

For survivors of cybercrime, the aftermath isn't just about financial restitution or even the apprehension of the perpetrators. It's about regaining a sense of control and safety in a world that, for a moment, felt unpredictable and malevolent.

Consider Jessica, a young professional whose personal images were maliciously disseminated online. While the immediate violation was devastating, the longer-term impact was profound. She battled anxiety, faced unsolicited judgment, and grappled with the unending fear of where those images might resurface next. Jessica's story is emblematic of countless others who face not just the direct consequences of cybercrimes, but also the cascading emotional and psychological impacts.

Voices of Resilience

Yet, as we delve deeper, we also discover the incredible resilience that many survivors display. For some, this resilience manifests in small, daily acts of defiance—like reclaiming their online presence or engaging in digital communities with renewed caution and wisdom.

Elena, for instance, was a victim of an online scam that preyed on her trust and generosity. Instead of retreating from the digital world, she channeled her experience into advocacy, educating others about online frauds and ensuring they don't fall for the same pitfalls.

The Path to Redemption

Beyond resilience, there's a journey of redemption. Some survivors harness their experiences to drive broader societal change. They become advocates, educators, and activists. They not only seek justice for themselves but work to prevent others from enduring similar traumas.

Take the case of Alex, a teenager who was cyberbullied to the brink of despair. With support and therapy, Alex managed to rebuild his life. But he didn't stop there. He initiated community dialogues on cyberbullying, bringing to light the silent epidemic many young people face and urging educational institutions to prioritize digital well-being.

Closure in a Digital World

In the digital age, closure takes on a new meaning. It's not just about healing but also about regaining faith in the digital realm—a space that offers as much promise as it does peril. Many survivors, in their journey of healing, embark on a quest to make the internet safer, kinder, and more accountable.

Concluding Reflections

As we listen to these voices, a profound realization emerges. The digital realm, despite its binaries, is deeply human. Every byte carries a story, every pixel echoes emotions. And while there are shadows, there's also an enduring light—the light of human tenacity, kindness, and an unwavering belief in redemption.

Through these narratives of impact and redemption, we're reminded that while technology evolves, the core human values of resilience, recovery, and renewal remain timeless. These stories inspire hope, affirming that even in the face of adversity, individuals can rise, heal, and in the process, transform the digital landscape for the better.

Chapter 8: Digital Demons: Real-Life Serial Files of Cybercrime

The internet has revolutionized the way we communicate, form relationships, and even fall in love. However, the anonymity and vastness of this digital realm have also given rise to a new breed of predators who exploit the medium's inherent vulnerabilities. These are individuals who didn't just stop at cyberbullying or online harassment—they took their malevolent intentions a step further, crossing the boundary from the virtual into the tangible, culminating in heinous real-world crimes. In this chapter, we delve into the chilling chronicles of ten such individuals who turned their online personas into instruments of real-life horror.

1. **John Edward Robinson:** Often dubbed the "Internet's first serial killer", Robinson exploited online chat rooms in the early days of the internet, luring women with promises of

employment or BDSM relationships. His crimes spanned from 1984 to 2000, with many of his victims met online in the latter years.

In the murky annals of cybercrime, few figures loom as large and as menacing as John Edward Robinson. With a criminal record stretching back to the 1960s, Robinson's transgressions began long before the advent of the World Wide Web. Yet, it was the emergence of the internet that allowed him to escalate his crimes to new, chilling heights.

Profile of a Predator:

Born in 1943, Robinson grew up in Cicero, Illinois. As a young adult, he was convicted of multiple minor crimes. However, by the time he reached middle age, he'd crafted an image of a respectable, community-involved family man, living with his wife and children in Kansas City.

The Digital Hunting Ground:

With the burgeoning internet of the 1990s, chat rooms became Robinson's preferred hunting grounds. The anonymity and trust inherent to these platforms allowed him to portray himself variously as a wealthy businessman, a benefactor, and sometimes even as a member of a secretive sadomasochistic cult. He offered vulnerable women promises — jobs, money, relationships, even the lure of a secretive BDSM lifestyle. And they believed him.

Victims Ensnared:

Over the span of nearly two decades, from 1984 to 2000, Robinson lured countless women into his web of deceit. While not all these encounters ended in murder, many did.

- **Lisa Stasi and her daughter Tiffany:** In 1985, Lisa, a young mother of a 4-month-old baby girl, disappeared mysteriously. Robinson, promising her a job and a fresh start, had wooed her. He then falsified documents and gave Tiffany to his brother, who, unaware of the nefarious proceedings, legally adopted her.

- **Izabela Lewicka:** A Polish immigrant and a former Purdue University student, Lewicka was promised a job and an engagement ring by Robinson. In 1999, she signed a 115-item slave contract that gave Robinson total control over her. Later that year, she disappeared.

- **Suzette Trouten:** A nurse from Michigan, Trouten was lured by the promise of a lucrative job caring for Robinson's ailing father. She too was never seen again after her meeting with him in 2000.

These are just a few names from the litany of Robinson's victims, each story more heart-wrenching than the last.

Unmasking the Monster:

It was the year 2000 when Robinson's reign of terror came to a screeching halt. Suspicions had been mounting, and law enforcement was closing in. A search of Robinson's 16-acre farm led to the gruesome discovery of two decaying bodies stored in barrels. Further searches in his storage facilities yielded more such barrels, each with a grim cargo within.

Confronted with overwhelming evidence, Robinson stood trial in Kansas in 2002, where he was convicted of three murders and sentenced to death. Later, in Missouri, he pleaded guilty to five more homicides and received multiple life sentences without the possibility of parole.

Legacy of Horror:

Robinson's crimes serve as a grim testament to the perils of the digital age. His ability to exploit the burgeoning internet to prey on the vulnerable underscores the importance of exercising caution in the virtual world. It also points to the dual nature of technology: while the internet has the power to connect and uplift, in the wrong hands, it can become a weapon of unparalleled cruelty.

2. **Stephen Port:** Known as the "Grindr Killer," Port targeted young gay men on the Grindr dating app between 2014 and 2015 in the UK. He administered lethal doses of date-rape drugs to his victims, causing their deaths.

Stephen Port: The Grindr Killer's Reign of Terror

In the expansive world of online dating, apps and websites have created unprecedented avenues for connections, both transient and lasting. However, as with all tools, they're only as benevolent as the hands wielding them. Enter Stephen Port, a man whose malevolent use of the popular dating app, Grindr, earned him the ominous moniker of the "Grindr Killer."

A Twisted Path:

Born in 1975 in Essex, Stephen Port lived a relatively unremarkable life in the London borough of Barking. A chef by profession, Port's quiet demeanor gave no outward signs of the darkness lurking within. However, beneath this facade was a man with sinister desires and an uncanny knack for exploiting the vulnerabilities of the digital age.

Predation in the Digital Age:

Between 2014 and 2015, Port used the Grindr dating app to target young gay men, luring them with the promise of companionship. For many of these young men, Grindr offered a discreet avenue to connect with like-minded individuals, away from the prying eyes of a society that was still grappling with accepting different sexual orientations. Port weaponized this trust.

His modus operandi was chilling: he would drug his victims using a lethal combination of date-rape drugs, rendering them unconscious. In this vulnerable state, Port would sexually assault them. The high doses of the drugs he administered often resulted in fatal overdoses.

The Lives Lost:

- **Anthony Walgate:** A fashion student and occasional escort, Anthony was Port's first known victim. His body was discovered outside Port's apartment in June 2014.

- **Gabriel Kovari:** Hailing from Slovakia, 22-year-old Gabriel was found dead in a graveyard near Port's home in August 2014.

- **Daniel Whitworth:** Only a month after Gabriel's death, another body was discovered in the same graveyard. It was Daniel Whitworth, a 21-year-old chef. A forged suicide note was found on him, seemingly written by Daniel, claiming responsibility for Gabriel's death and expressing guilt.

- **Jack Taylor:** A forklift operator, Jack was Port's final known victim. His body was found in September 2015, again near the same graveyard.

Justice Served:

Suspicion began to mount as the bodies piled up, all in close proximity to Port's residence. Inconsistencies in the stories and evidence, especially the dubious suicide note found on Daniel Whitworth, drew investigators' attention to Port.

In 2016, Stephen Port stood trial, charged with the murders of the four young men. The weight of the evidence was overwhelming, and Port was convicted on all counts. He was sentenced to life in prison with no chance of parole.

A Digital Cautionary Tale:

Stephen Port's gruesome crimes underscore the perils lurking within the promise of digital connections. While the vast majority of online encounters are harmless, even fruitful, the story of the Grindr Killer is a chilling reminder that evil can lurk just a click away. As our lives become increasingly intertwined with the digital realm, the tale of Stephen Port stands as a stark warning of the need for vigilance and caution in the online world.

3. **David Heiss:** Obsessed with a girl he met on an online gaming site, Heiss traveled from Germany to the UK in 2008 and fatally stabbed the girl's boyfriend out of jealousy.

In the dark recesses of the internet, where virtual worlds intertwine with reality, a sinister tale of obsession and jealousy unfolds. David Heiss, a seemingly unassuming individual from Germany, would become a name forever associated with a heinous crime that rocked the online gaming community and left a trail of tragedy in its wake.

David Heiss's story began innocently enough, navigating the intricate landscapes of online gaming sites in search of companionship and connection. It was on one of these platforms that he crossed paths with a young woman whose virtual presence captivated him. As days turned into weeks and messages evolved into conversations, Heiss found himself entangled in a web of infatuation. The girl, who hailed from the United Kingdom, had a boyfriend - a detail that would prove to be the catalyst for a grim sequence of events.

As Heiss's feelings deepened, his obsession evolved into an all-consuming force that clouded his judgment and corroded his sense of reality. The virtual world he inhabited with the girl became more significant to him than the real one. Consumed by jealousy and fueled by his unchecked emotions, Heiss decided to take drastic measures to eliminate the perceived obstacle standing between him and his online crush.

In 2008, Heiss made a fateful decision that would change multiple lives forever. He boarded a plane from Germany to the United Kingdom, driven by a mixture of desperation and determination. His goal was to confront the girl's boyfriend, the embodiment of his frustration and envy. Armed with a knife and consumed by a volatile mix of emotions, Heiss tracked down his unsuspecting victim and confronted him face-to-face.

The details of that chilling encounter remain etched in the annals of crime history. In a fit of jealous rage, Heiss unleashed a savage attack on the girl's boyfriend, fatally stabbing him. The crime sent shockwaves through the online gaming community and beyond, as the tragic consequences of an unchecked obsession became painfully evident.

However, Heiss's reign of terror was short-lived. The authorities swiftly apprehended him, and he was subsequently put on trial for his gruesome act. As the details of his obsession, the murder, and the disturbing path that led him to commit such a heinous act emerged in the courtroom, the chilling narrative of his obsession took center stage.

In the aftermath of the trial, Heiss's motivations were scrutinized by psychologists, criminologists, and society at large. The case served as a grim reminder of the potential dangers lurking in the digital realm, where connections formed behind screens can sometimes have profound real-world implications. It shed light on the dark consequences of unchecked obsessions and the fragile line between fantasy and reality.

Ultimately, Heiss's story serves as a haunting cautionary tale, highlighting the devastating impact of obsession and jealousy. His actions not only ended the life of an innocent young man but also shattered the lives of those connected to him. It stands as a somber reminder of the dangers that can arise when unchecked emotions spiral out of control, blurring the boundaries between the virtual and the real in the most tragic and irreversible of ways.

4. **Mark Twitchell:** Inspired by the TV show "Dexter," this aspiring filmmaker lured his victims using online dating sites. He killed and dismembered a man in 2008, allegedly as research for a movie script.

In the shadowy intersection of fiction and reality, the harrowing story of Mark Twitchell unfolds, a chilling narrative that blurs the line between a fan's admiration for a TV show and a descent into darkness that culminated in real-life horror. The tale delves into the mind of a man whose obsession with a fictional serial killer led him down a path of twisted emulation and heinous crimes.

Mark Twitchell's story is one that eerily mirrors the premise of the television series "Dexter," a show that chronicles the life of a vigilante serial killer who meticulously targets and eliminates other murderers.

Yet, for Twitchell, the line between inspiration and emulation became disturbingly indistinct, ultimately leading to a series of gruesome crimes that would shock the world.

In 2008, Twitchell, an aspiring filmmaker from Edmonton, Canada, found himself captivated by the character Dexter Morgan, the titular character of the popular TV series. As he immersed himself in the show's dark narrative, something within him shifted, and the fictional boundaries of Dexter's world began to blend with his own. What started as a fascination with a fictional anti-hero soon evolved into a sinister obsession.

Armed with a twisted vision, Twitchell turned to the anonymity of online dating sites to satisfy his insidious desires. Posing as a charismatic and charming persona, he lured unsuspecting men into his web, promising exciting encounters and connections. These interactions, however, were merely a prelude to his sinister intentions.

In a chilling parallel to Dexter's methods, Twitchell meticulously planned his acts of violence. In 2008, he successfully lured Johnny Altinger, a man he met on an online dating site, to a rented garage under the guise of a romantic liaison. Once Altinger arrived, the trap was sprung. Twitchell attacked and killed his victim, carrying out acts of brutality that mirrored the very show that had inspired him.

What followed was a macabre sequence of events that would defy comprehension. Twitchell dismembered Altinger's body and disposed of the remains in a truly horrifying manner. As if he were scripting scenes for his films, he meticulously covered his tracks, attempting to erase any evidence that could lead back to him.

However, the darkness that Twitchell had embraced was not destined to remain hidden. A combination of forensic evidence, digital footprints, and the suspicious disappearance of Altinger set off alarm bells among law enforcement. Their investigation led them to the rented garage, where they uncovered a scene of unspeakable horror.

Twitchell's dual life was laid bare, as investigators unraveled the chilling tale of how a TV show's portrayal of vigilantism had taken root in his psyche, propelling him to commit acts that echoed the very horrors he had absorbed through the screen. His arrest, trial, and subsequent conviction marked the end of his reign of terror, revealing the depths of his depravity.

The case of Mark Twitchell stands as a stark reminder of the power of media to influence vulnerable minds and the dangerous consequences of unchecked obsessions. His attempt to emulate a fictional character's dark deeds led him down a treacherous path, forever intertwining his life with the very darkness he sought to replicate. The tragic fate of Johnny Altinger serves as a somber reminder of the devastating impact that such obsessions can have on innocent lives, as fiction turned to a horrifying reality with chilling and irreversible consequences.

5. **Alyssa Bustamante:** While not a serial killer, this teenager's online presence is noteworthy. She mentioned her urge to kill in her online

diary, and in 2009, she murdered her 9-year-old neighbor.

In the age of digital connectivity, the boundaries between the online world and real-life actions can blur with chilling consequences. The haunting story of Alyssa Bustamante serves as a grim reminder of how the internet can become a window into the darkest corners of a troubled mind, culminating in a shocking act that shattered a community's sense of safety.

Alyssa Bustamante's journey into infamy began in the virtual realm, where her online diary provided a disturbing glimpse into the depths of her psyche. In the era of the late 2000s, when social media and personal blogs reigned supreme, Bustamante's digital footprint would become a chilling precursor to a tragic event that would leave a lasting mark on the small town of St. Martins, Missouri.

Through her online diary, Bustamante shared her innermost thoughts, feelings, and disturbing inclinations. In these virtual confessions, she openly discussed an unsettling urge to kill, offering a disturbing insight into the turmoil brewing within her young mind.

In 2009, the tranquility of St. Martins was shattered when Bustamante's online musings translated into real-life horror. On a fateful day, the 15-year-old lured her 9-year-old neighbor, Elizabeth Olten, into the woods under the pretense of playing together. What followed was a gruesome act that defied comprehension and sent shockwaves through the community.

In a chilling and calculated act, Bustamante brutally murdered Elizabeth, robbing her of her innocent life and leaving a community in mourning. The brutality of the crime and the shocking revelation of Bustamante's true nature left the town in disbelief, struggling to reconcile the heinous act with the young girl they thought they knew.

As the investigation unfolded, Bustamante's online diary became a crucial piece of evidence, providing a disturbing backdrop to the crime. Her words, written in the digital realm, had morphed into a nightmarish reality that forever altered the lives of both the victim's family and her own.

The case shook the nation as details emerged in court, revealing a deeply troubled young woman grappling with a darkness that transcended the boundaries of her online presence. Bustamante's motives remained enigmatic; whether the murder was fueled by a genuine compulsion to fulfill her chilling urges or driven by a desire to experience the power and control she had fantasized about online, the tragedy left an indelible scar on all those involved.

In the aftermath, Bustamante was arrested, tried, and ultimately convicted for the murder of Elizabeth Olten. Her online diary, once a digital confessional, became a haunting testament to the dangers of overlooking warning signs and underestimating the potential gravity of online declarations.

The case of Alyssa Bustamante serves as a chilling reminder of the complex interplay between the digital and the real, and how the darkest corners of the mind can find expression through the anonymity and detachment of the online world. The tragedy stands as a cautionary tale, underscoring the need for vigilance and empathy, and the importance of addressing the signs of turmoil before they escalate into irreversible horrors that forever alter lives and communities.

6. **The Chatroom Stalker:** "Sarah" became infatuated with men she met in chat rooms, tracking them down in real life and killing those who didn't reciprocate her feelings.

In the hidden corners of the digital world, where identities blur and connections form through the glow of screens, the chilling saga of the Chatroom Stalker unfolds—a haunting narrative that blurs the lines between the virtual and the real, and showcases the sinister potential that lies within the shadows of the internet.

At first glance, "Sarah" appeared to be just another anonymous presence in the vast expanse of online chat rooms, where individuals from all walks of life could connect and share their thoughts. Beneath her seemingly innocuous facade, however, lay a mind veiled in obsession and driven by dark desires. This fictionalized tale explores the depths of her twisted psyche and the terrifying consequences that follow.

As the Chatroom Stalker, Sarah's digital persona was a masterful mask, concealing her true intent while she crafted a web of deceit that ensnared men in her virtual embrace. She used her charm and allure to forge connections, drawing unsuspecting victims into her online lair with promises of friendship and affection. But beneath the virtual façade lay a dangerous obsession that would soon spill over into the real world.

Sarah's fixation on these men transformed into a toxic infatuation that knew no bounds. Fueled by her insatiable need for reciprocation, she embarked on a chilling campaign of tracking down her chatroom companions in the physical realm. Armed with knowledge gleaned from their online interactions, she managed to identify their real-world identities, circumventing the barriers between the virtual and the tangible.

However, Sarah's twisted fantasy took a sinister turn when the boundaries between her online persona and her real-life actions dissolved completely. Faced with the realization that her affections were unrequited, her obsession warped into a deadly rage. The screen names that had once brought her fleeting moments of euphoria became targets, and her search turned into a hunt fueled by dark intentions.

In the shadowy corners of dark alleys and unsuspecting neighborhoods, Sarah's victims met their gruesome fate. Each man who failed to reciprocate her feelings became a casualty of her twisted desires, succumbing to a gruesome end at her hands. The chilling precision with which she carried out her acts left law enforcement baffled, as they struggled to link the escalating trail of deaths to a single elusive figure hiding behind the anonymity of the internet.

The Chatroom Stalker's reign of terror reached its climax in a showdown that tested the limits of law enforcement's capabilities and showcased the eerie potential of the online realm to blur the lines of reality. As investigators delved into the labyrinth of her digital footprint, they unraveled a disturbing narrative that spanned chat logs, messages, and the darkest corners of the human psyche.

The tale of the Chatroom Stalker stands as a chilling cautionary tale, a reminder of the dangers that lurk beneath the surface of the virtual world. It serves as a reminder that behind every screen name and online profile, real lives and emotions are at stake. As society grapples with the ever-expanding realm of digital connectivity, this fictionalized story forces us to confront the sinister potential that can emerge when the boundaries between the digital and the tangible are eroded, leading to a nightmarish reality that forever shatters lives and communities.

7. **The Digital Photographer:** "Jake" posed as a photographer online, luring aspiring models to

secluded locations where he'd assault and kill them.

In the age of social media's glossy allure and the promise of virtual connections, the fictionalized tale of the Digital Photographer unveils a chilling narrative of deception and horror. A man known only as "Jake" navigates the realm of pixels and profiles to ensnare unsuspecting aspiring models, leading them to a terrifying fate in remote locations far from the glamor they once sought.

Behind the veneer of a charismatic and talented photographer, Jake weaves a web of lies that draws in individuals yearning for their shot at the spotlight. With an impressive portfolio showcasing captivating portraits and stunning landscapes, he gains the trust of budding models eager to make their mark. But his true intentions are far from artistic; they're sinister, depraved, and deadly.

Jake's digital persona becomes a seductive mask that conceals his dark desires. He lures his unsuspecting victims into his trap through the allure of photoshoot opportunities, promising them the chance to elevate their careers and bask in the spotlight's glow. Aspiring models, drawn by the allure of fame and recognition, find themselves captivated by the promise of collaborating with a seemingly reputable photographer.

However, as the models arrive at the designated secluded locations, the veneer of professionalism shatters, and the sinister truth is unveiled. The picturesque landscapes that were meant to frame their dreams become the backdrop for their nightmares. Jake's charismatic façade crumbles, revealing a predator driven by sinister motives that transcend the realm of photography.

In a chilling orchestration, the Digital Photographer's true intent surfaces. The idyllic surroundings become haunting stages for acts of brutality. As his victims realize the deception, they are already ensnared in a deadly game of survival. With a cold and calculated demeanor, Jake assaults and ultimately kills his prey, leaving their dreams shattered in his wake.

The Digital Photographer's sinister spree leaves a trail of shattered lives and communities in its wake. As law enforcement struggles to piece together the fragmented puzzle, the haunting realization sets in: the digital world's allure can mask the darkest intentions. Unraveling the web of deceit that Jake has spun proves to be a daunting task, as the anonymity of the online realm shrouds his true identity.

The tale of the Digital Photographer serves as a haunting reminder of the precarious nature of online interactions and the chilling potential of individuals who manipulate the virtual world for their own sinister ends. It underscores the importance of vigilance in the digital age, urging us to question and verify the motives of those we encounter online.

In a world where appearances can be deceiving and connections can be forged through the mere click of a button, the fictionalized narrative of the Digital Photographer serves as a grim testament to the darkness that can fester beneath the surface. It prompts us to tread carefully in the vast expanse of the digital landscape, where shadows and secrets may lurk just beyond the glow of our screens.

8. The Craigslist Killer

The Craigslist Killer, whose real name is Philip Markoff, was a medical student who gained notoriety for a series of crimes related to Craigslist advertisements. He targeted women who had posted ads offering massage services, and his actions shocked the nation as details of his crimes emerged.

Philip Markoff's victims and the dates of his crimes are as follows:

1. **Julissa Brisman**: Markoff's first known victim, Julissa Brisman, was a 25-year-old woman from New York who had advertised massage services on Craigslist. On April 14, 2009, Markoff allegedly responded to her ad and arranged a meeting at the Marriott Copley Place Hotel in Boston. During the encounter, he allegedly attacked and fatally shot Brisman. She was found dead in her hotel room.

2. **Trisha Leffler**: On April 10, 2009, just days before the murder of Julissa Brisman, Markoff allegedly targeted another woman, Trisha Leffler, who had also advertised massage services on Craigslist. The attack took place at the Westin Copley Place Hotel in Boston. Leffler was restrained and robbed, but she managed to escape and notify the authorities.

3. **Corinne Stout**: While Corinne Stout was not physically harmed, she was another potential victim of Philip Markoff's crimes. She had also advertised massage services on Craigslist and had exchanged emails with Markoff. They had arranged to meet, but Stout canceled the meeting after hearing about the attacks on Brisman and Leffler. This incident prompted the police to search Markoff's apartment.

Philip Markoff was arrested on April 20, 2009, after evidence from surveillance footage and electronic communications linked him to the crimes. He was charged with the murder of Julissa Brisman, as well as other offenses related to the attacks on Trisha Leffler and Corinne Stout.

The Craigslist Killer case shocked the public and highlighted the potential dangers of online interactions. Markoff's arrest and subsequent suicide in jail in 2010 added to the mystery and intrigue surrounding the case, leaving unanswered questions about his motives and the extent of his crimes.

9. **The Gaming Avenger:** "Liam" held grudges in the virtual gaming world. Taking it beyond the screen, he tracked down his online "enemies," violently confronting them in reality.

In the realm where pixels and avatars come alive, the chilling saga of the Gaming Avenger unfolds—a twisted narrative that transcends the confines of the virtual gaming world to manifest in brutal, real-life confrontations. Behind the screen name "Liam," a sinister figure navigates the blurred boundaries between fantasy and reality, driven by digital grudges that erupt into a series of shocking and violent acts.

At first glance, Liam appears to be just another gamer immersed in the intricate landscapes of virtual realms. However, beneath the veil of anonymity, a dangerous obsession takes root. This fictional tale delves into the psyche of the Gaming Avenger, a character whose thirst for revenge knows no bounds and whose actions send ripples of fear through the online gaming community.

The Gaming Avenger's digital grudges are not mere frustrations left on the gaming server. For him, the victories and defeats within the virtual world translate into deeply personal vendettas that demand real-world reckoning. Fueled by perceived slights and virtual betrayals, he crosses the line from gaming rivalries to a chilling campaign of tracking down his online "enemies" in the physical world.

As the Gaming Avenger's virtual clashes intensify, so do his real-world tactics. Armed with the information gleaned from online interactions, he becomes a digital detective of sorts, piecing together his enemies' identities and locations. The line between pixels and pavement blurs as he embarks on a twisted mission to confront and punish those he deems responsible for his online grievances.

The Gaming Avenger's confrontations extend far beyond the digital realm. He tracks down his victims to their homes, workplaces, and public spaces, delivering a grim reality check that shatters the illusion of distance provided by the screen. With a chilling determination, he subjects his victims to violent confrontations that mirror the intensity of the virtual battles they once engaged in.

The impact of the Gaming Avenger's actions reverberates through the online gaming community, as players become hyper-aware of the potential real-life consequences of their in-game actions. Law enforcement struggles to contain the chaos, grappling with the challenges posed by a figure who operates in both the virtual and physical worlds.

The tale of the Gaming Avenger is a cautionary reminder of the powerful emotions that can be stoked by the virtual interactions we engage in daily. It underscores the importance of empathy, respect, and the awareness that even behind the screen, real people with real emotions are at play. As society becomes increasingly intertwined with the digital landscape, the boundaries between the real and the virtual blur, highlighting the urgency of understanding the implications of our actions, whether they occur within lines of code or on city streets.

10. **The Online Confesso:** "Clara" would befriend her victims online, coaxing dark secrets out of them. If she deemed them "unworthy," she'd hunt them down, believing she was enacting justice.

In the hidden recesses of the internet, where connections form through the veil of anonymity, the haunting narrative of the Online Confessor unfolds—a chilling story that blurs the lines between empathy and vengeance. Under the guise of the online persona "Clara," a mysterious figure traverses the digital realm, manipulating confidences into a deadly game of perceived justice.

Clara's digital presence is deceptively unassuming, drawing individuals into her virtual embrace with a comforting ear and an empathetic demeanor. However, beneath her veneer of sympathy, a dark and twisted agenda takes shape. This fictionalized story delves into the psyche of the Online Confessor, an enigmatic figure who believes herself to be an arbiter of morality in the digital age.

The Online Confessor's web of deceit extends beyond the superficial boundaries of the online realm. As she befriends her victims, she employs an uncanny ability to coax their deepest, darkest secrets from them. Her digital charm and apparent empathy mask her true intent—to judge their actions according to her own twisted standards of morality.

For Clara, the threshold between virtual connection and real-world retribution blurs significantly. After extracting the secrets that lay dormant within her victims, she proceeds to judge their worthiness, deciding whether their actions deserve punishment. In her distorted perspective, she deems herself a self-appointed agent of justice, destined to enact retribution for the wrongs she believes have been committed.

When Clara concludes that her victims are "unworthy," her digital vendetta takes a chilling turn. Armed with the information she's gathered, she embarks on a hunt to track down those who have crossed her moral boundaries. The Online Confessor transforms into a real-world avenger, fueled by a twisted sense of duty to deliver her version of punishment.

The trail of the Online Confessor is a web of intrigue and danger. Law enforcement grapples with the challenge of identifying the source of these vendettas that unfold in both the digital and physical worlds. As victims fall prey to Clara's quest for justice, a sense of dread permeates the online communities where friendships once flourished.

The tale of the Online Confessor is a haunting reminder of the power and peril of online interactions. It underscores the potential consequences of our digital interactions and the fragility of the barriers that separate the virtual from the real. As society navigates the intricacies of digital connections, it serves as a stark reminder that behind every profile lies a person with secrets, emotions, and a humanity that should never be lost in the shadowy landscape of the internet.

Concluding Reflections:

The cases above highlight the potential dangers lurking in the vast expanse of the internet. While the web has undoubtedly been a boon, enabling connections and relationships across geographical boundaries, these tales serve as a grim reminder that not all online interactions are benign.

In a world increasingly moving towards digital interactions, it's imperative to tread with caution, be aware of the risks, and ensure we protect ourselves and our loved ones from the dark recesses of the virtual realm. The tragedies of those who've suffered at the hands of online predators should serve as a wake-up call to all about the importance of digital safety and awareness.

Conclusion: Unbroken Chains

Our journey through the intricate web of the digital world, painted with shadows of true crime, has been both harrowing and enlightening. As we ventured into the depths of cybercrime's abyss, the stories we encountered were not just about technology, anonymity, or deceit. They were, at their core, human stories—tales of resilience, frailty, ingenuity, and endurance.

Lessons from the Abyss

From exploring the digital underworld, several profound truths have emerged. First and foremost, as technology continues its relentless advance, so does the nature of crime. The digital age, with its boundless opportunities, also harbors dark corners where malevolence lurks. Understanding this duality is crucial for any individual or institution navigating the online world.

However, this exploration also underscored a timeless lesson: the most effective weapon against darkness isn't necessarily more technology, but the persistent light of human vigilance, education, and cooperation. It's about communities coming together, individuals staying informed, and societies maintaining a dialogue on the ethical implications of our ever-evolving digital interactions.

The Unbreakable Human Spirit

Amidst the tales of deception and malevolence, glimmers of hope persist. These beacons of resilience are the survivors—individuals who, despite enduring unimaginable adversities in the digital realm, emerge stronger, wiser, and often determined to prevent others from facing the same perils. Their stories remind us of the indomitable spirit within each of us, a spirit that refuses to be defeated by shadows, whether they emerge from the physical or digital world.

Equally inspiring is the unwavering dedication of law enforcement agencies, cybersecurity experts, and digital guardians who work tirelessly to make the online world safer. Their commitment, often forged in the crucible of challenging investigations and complex digital labyrinths, is a testament to humanity's collective determination to protect and persevere.

Moreover, the digital realm's vastness, often perceived as a challenge, can also be its strength. It enables global communities to unite, share knowledge, and collectively combat the threats that loom. This interconnectedness, when harnessed with intent and unity, can be a formidable force against cyber adversaries.

Charting the Way Forward

As we reflect on our journey through the nexus of true crime and cybercrime, it's essential to remember that these narratives aren't just tales of caution but also of empowerment. With every challenge the digital age presents, there arises an opportunity—to learn, to adapt, and to fortify our defenses.

The chains that bind humanity—of compassion, resilience, and shared purpose—remain unbroken, even in the face of evolving adversities. By cherishing these bonds and understanding the lessons from the abyss, we

can ensure that the digital age, for all its complexities,
remains a realm of promise, potential, and hope.

Epilogue: Into the Shadows

Epilogue: Into the Shadows

As the chapters of these chilling narratives close, we find ourselves peering into the future—an uncertain landscape where the evolution of technology casts new shadows upon the canvas of crime, investigation, and justice. The digital age has ushered in a world of unprecedented connectivity and convenience, but it has also unveiled a realm of darker possibilities, where the line between the virtual and the real becomes increasingly blurred.

The Future of Disappearances:

In the crystal ball of technology, we glimpse a future shaped by the convergence of innovation and malice. Crimes, once confined to physical spaces, now traverse the digital divide, leaving an intricate trail of data that both aids and challenges law enforcement. The dark artistry of disappearance may evolve, merging virtual subterfuge with tangible vanishings.

Advanced surveillance technologies may provide unprecedented insights into a suspect's digital footprint, reconstructing their every move through geolocation data, online interactions, and biometric identifiers. However, as technologies evolve, so do the tactics of those who wish to remain unseen. Cryptocurrencies, anonymizing tools, and the dark web may further obscure the paths of criminals, creating an intricate dance of digital cat and mouse.

Virtual realities and augmented realms may offer new canvases for malevolent acts, where boundaries between real and simulated experiences blur. Crimes might transcend the physical world, testing the very limits of our understanding of crime scenes, evidence, and culpability.

A Call to Vigilance:

In the face of these looming shadows, there emerges a call to vigilance—a plea to wield our newfound knowledge as a shield against the invisible dangers that lurk. The lessons learned from these stories are not mere entertainment; they are windows into the complexities of human nature and the potential dangers that arise when technology and malice intertwine.

As we navigate the intricate landscape of the digital age, it is imperative that we remain vigilant guardians of our personal information, cautious participants in online interactions, and critical consumers of digital media. We must recognize that the online world is not devoid of consequences; it is merely a reflection of the real one, carrying the same capacity for both good and evil.

By understanding the risks posed by the virtual realm, we empower ourselves to make informed choices, both as individuals and as a society. We become active participants in the evolution of law enforcement techniques and digital security measures. We foster a culture where empathy and respect transcend screens and pixels, reminding us that behind every online persona lies a person with dreams, fears, and a humanity that demands recognition.

So, as we step away from these fictionalized tales and reenter the real world, let us carry with us the cautionary whispers from the shadows. Let us weave threads of empathy and understanding in the digital tapestry we collectively create. And let us remember that the lessons of the past can illuminate the path forward, guiding us away from the abyss of darkness and into a future where the promise of technology can be harnessed for the betterment of humanity.

www.ingramcontent.com/pod-product-compliance
Lightning Source LLC
Chambersburg PA
CBHW031305250726

48656CB00005B/1647